Embellishment
Stitch Guide

CONTENTS

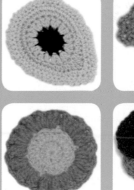

LEISURE ARTS, INC.
Maumelle, Arkansas

D0018073

PRODUCED BY:

PRODUCTION TEAM:

Creative Directors: Jean Leinhauser and Rita Weiss
Technical Editor: Susan Lowman
Photographer: Carol Wilson Mansfield
Book Design: Joyce Lerner

Diagrams © 2016 by The Creative Partners™ LLC

PUBLISHED BY:

Library of Congress Control Number: 2015955191
ISBN-13: 978-1-4647-3885-2

A Note from Jean

In this book you will find everything from glittering tassels to braids used in vintage Romanian lace to a heart motif you can sew on your sleeve.

Each chapter introduces another group of crocheted embellishments designed to add a special flair to your crocheted or knitted projects.

If you're looking for a ruffled border for an afghan for your little princess, or a big red rose to accent your suit jacket, you will find it in these pages.

As you read through the patterns you'll notice a few things that are missing: most of the projects have no materials lists, and no hook or gauge specification. That's because you can work the patterns in any yarn you choose—from fine crochet cotton to bulky chenille—with any size hook that gives the effect you want.

Different yarns will give very different looks. The photo shows how one of our braids takes on a completely different personality when worked in size 3 crochet cotton, in sport weight yarn, and in worsted weight yarn. **Note:** *The instructions are Braid 11 on page 57.*

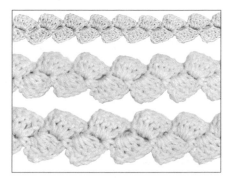

Except for the cords and braids, which we made in size 3 crochet cotton, the projects are all shown worked in sport or dk weight yarn. But you can have fun experimenting with different yarn textures and colors to create embellishments that are uniquely you.

And in case you can't remember how to crochet, or if you are confused about what those abbreviations and symbols mean, spend a little time with our Refresher Course starting on page 86. Then you'll be ready to start embellishing.

Jean Leinhauser, Creative Partners, LLC

FLOWERS & LEAVES

Flowers and leaves are fun to make, and are a great way to use up scrap yarn. The flowers are good for wearing as pins (craft stores carry pin backs to which you can attach the flowers), or as decorations for packages or clothing.

A small flower is a sweet addition
to a child's dress or sweater.
A group of flowers looks wonderful
on a crocheted purse, or on a hat.
A big flower on a curtain tieback adds
drama. Our flowers are not botanically
correct, so feel free to change their colors.
Where there are flowers, there must be
leaves, so we've given you a selection
of various shapes and sizes.

FLOWERS

Pink Bloom

Three colors:
Color A (yellow)
Color B (deep pink)
Color C (med pink)

Instructions

With Color A, ch 6, join with sl st to form a ring.

Rnd 1 (right side): Ch 5 (counts as a dc and ch-2 sp), dc in ring; (ch 2, dc in ring) 4 times, ch 2; join with sl st in 3rd ch of beg ch-5.

Rnd 2: Ch 1; *in next ch-2 sp work (sc, hdc, 3 dc, hdc, sc): petal made; rep from * around; join with sl st in beg sc. Finish off Color A.

Rnd 3: Turn piece to wrong side. Join Color B with sl st in back strands of center dc in any petal; *ch 4, sl st in back strands of center dc of next petal; rep from * around, ending last rep with ch 4; join in beg sl st, ch 1, turn piece to right side.

Rnd 4: *In next ch-4 sp work (sc, hdc, 2 dc, 1 tr, 2 dc, hdc, sc): petal made; rep from * around; join in beg sc. Finish off Color B.

Rnd 5: Turn piece to wrong side. Join Color C with sl st in back strands of tr of any petal; *ch 5, sl st in back strands of center tr of next petal; rep from * around, ending last rep with ch 5; join in beg sl st; ch 1, turn piece to right side.

Rnd 6: *In next ch-5 sp work 8 sc; rep from * around; join with sc in beg sc.

Rnd 7: With right side facing, *ch 3 (equals a dc), dc in next sc, (ch 1, tr in next sc) 4 times, ch 1, dc in next sc, ch 3, sc in next sc; rep from * around; join in beg sc. Finish off; weave in yarn ends.

Marigold

Two colors:
Color A (gold)
Color B (orange)

Stitch Guide
Cluster (CL): *YO, insert hook in specified lp and draw up a lp to height of a dc; YO and draw through 2 lps on hook; rep from * 2 times more in same lp, YO and draw through 4 lps: CL made.

Instructions
Rnd 1: With Color A, ch 4; work 11 dc in 4th ch from hook; join with sl st in top of beg ch: 12 dc.

Rnd 2: Ch 3 (counts as a dc), dc in base of ch; work 2 dc in each dc around; join with sc in top of beg ch: 24 dc.

Rnd 3: *Ch 3, skip 3 dc, sc in next dc; rep from * around, ending last rep with ch 3; join with sl st in beg sc: 6 ch-3 sps. Finish off Color A.

Rnd 4: Join Color B with sc in any ch-3 lp; ch 3, CL in same lp; (ch 3, CL in same lp) 2 times more; ch 3; * in next ch-3 lp work (CL, ch 3) 3 times; rep from * around; join with sl st in top of beg CL. Finish off Color B; weave in yarn ends.

Forget-Me-Not

Two colors:
Color A (yellow)
Color B (blue)

Instructions
With Color A, ch 5; join with sl st to form a ring.

Rnd 1: Ch 1, work 10 sc in ring; join with sl st in beg sc; finish off Color A.

Rnd 2: Join Color B with sl st in any sc; in same sc work (ch 3, 2 dc, ch 3, sl st), skip next sc; *in next sc work (sl st, ch 3, 2 dc, ch 3, sl st), skip next sc; rep from * 3 times more: 5 petals made; join with sl st in beg sl st. Finish off; weave in yarn ends.

Fancy Flora

Instructions
Ch 4, join with sl st to form a ring.

Rnd 1: Ch 3 (counts as a dc), work 9 dc in ring: 10 dc; join with sc in 3rd ch of beg ch-3.

Rnd 2: Sc in each dc around: 10 sc; join in beg sc. **Note:** Work will tend to turn to wrong side; push so right side is facing you.

Rnd 3: *Ch 2, skip next sc, sc in next sc; rep from * around, ending last rep with ch 2; join in beg sc: 5 ch-2 sps.

Rnd 4: In each ch-2 sp work petal of (sl st, ch 2, 4 dc, ch 2, sl st); join in beg sl st: 5 petals made.

Rnd 5: Ch 1; working behind petals of Rnd 4, *sc in back lp of next skipped sc on Rnd 3, ch 4; rep from * around; join in beg sc: 5 ch-4 lps.

Rnd 6: In each ch-4 lp work petal of (sl st, ch 2, 7 dc, ch 2, sl st): 5 petals made; join in beg sl st.

Rnd 7: Ch 2; working behind petals of Rnd 6, *sl st in back strands of center dc of next petal on Rnd 6, ch 5; rep from * around; join in beg sl st.

Rnd 8: In each ch-5 lp work petal of (sl st, ch 2, 9 dc, ch 2, sl st); join in beg sl st: 5 petals made. Finish off; weave in yarn ends.

Cornflower

Instructions

With Color A, ch 6, join with sl st to form a ring.

Rnd 1: Ch 1; in ring work (sc, ch 2) 8 times; join in beg sc; finish off Color A.

Rnd 2: Join Color B with sl st in any ch-2 sp; ch 3 (counts as a dc), 3 dc in same sp; ch 3, turn; dc in first dc (at base of turning ch), dc in next 2 dc and in top of beg ch-3: 5-dc petal made; ch 3, turn; *working behind petal just made, work 4 dc in next ch-2 sp, ch 3, turn; dc in first dc (at base of turning ch), dc in next 3 dc: 5-dc petal made; ch 3, turn; rep from * around, ending last rep with join with sl st in top of beg ch-3. Finish off; weave in yarn ends.

Two colors:
Color A (yellow)
Color B (med blue)

Ruffled Blossom

Rnd 3: *Ch 3, sl st in next st; rep from * around; join in beg sl st. Finish off; weave in yarn ends.

Cockscomb

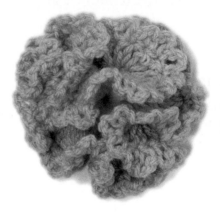

Two colors:
Color A (orange)
Color B (gold)

Instructions

With Color A, ch 6, join with sl st to form a ring.

Rnd 1: Ch 5 (counts as a dc and ch-2 sp), dc in ring; *ch 2, dc in ring; rep from * 4 times more, ch 2; join with sl st in 3rd ch of beg ch-5: 6 ch-2 sps. Finish off Color A.

Rnd 2: Join Color B with sl st in any ch-2 sp; ch 1, in same sp work (sc, hdc, 3 dc, hdc, sc); *in next ch-2 sp work (sc, hdc, 3 dc, hdc, sc); rep from * around; join with sl st in beg sc.

Two colors:
Color A (yellow)
Color B (pink)

Instructions

With Color A, ch 4, join with sl st to form a ring.

Rnd 1: Ch 1, work 6 sc in ring; do not join.

Rnd 2: Work 2 sc in each sc: 12 sc; join with sl st in beg sc; finish off Color A.

Rnd 3: Join Color B with sl st in any sc; ch 1, work 3 sc in same sc as joining and in each rem sc: 36 sc; join with sl st in beg sc.

Rnd 4: Ch 3, dc in joining; work 2 dc in each rem sc: 72 dc; join with sc in top of beg ch-3.

Rnd 5: *Ch 3, sc in next dc; rep from * around, ending with ch 3; join in top of beg ch-3. Finish off; weave in yarn ends.

Royal Rose

Instructions
Ch 5, join with sl st to form a ring.

Rnd 1 (right side): *In ring work (sc, 3 dc, sc): petal made; rep from * 3 times more: 4 petals made; join with sl st in beg sc.

Rnd 2: Ch 1; *working behind petals of Rnd 1, sc in back strands of first sc of next petal, ch 4, sc in back strands of last sc of same petal; rep from * 3 times more; join with sl st in beg sc: 4 ch-4 lps.

Rnd 3: *In next ch-4 lp work (sc, dc, tr, dc, sc, dc, tr, dc, sc): 2 petals made; rep from * 3 times more: 8 petals made; do not join.

Rnd 4: Working behind petals of Rnd 3, sc in back strands of first sc of next petal; *ch 4, sc in back strands of next sc; rep from * around, ending last rep with ch 4; join with sl st in beg sc: 8 ch-4 lps.

Rnd 5: *In next ch-4 lp work (sl st, ch 3, 4 dc, ch 3, sl st): petal made; rep from * around; join with sl st in beg sl st: 8 petals made. Finish off; weave in yarn ends.

A Little Lavender

Two Colors:
Color A (off white)
Color B (lavender)

Instructions

With Color A, ch 6, join with sl st to form a ring.

Rnd 1 (right side): *In ring work (sc, 4 dc, sc): petal made; rep from * twice more; join with sl st in beg sc: 3 petals made.

Rnd 2: Ch 2; working behind petals, *sc in back strands of center 2 dc sts of next petal; ch 3, sc in back strands of next sc; ch 3; rep from * around: 6 ch-3 sps; join with sc in beg sc.

Rnd 3: *In next ch-3 sp work petal of (sl st, ch 3, 5 dc, ch 3, sl st), sc in next sc; rep from * around; join with sl st in beg sl st.

Rnd 4: Working behind petals of Rnd 3, sc around next sc of Rnd 2; ch 6, *sc around next sc, ch 6; rep from * around: 6 ch-6 sps; join.

Rnd 5: *In next ch-6 sp work (sl st, ch 3, 7 dc, ch 3, sl st), sc in next sc; rep from * around; join. Finish off; weave in yarn ends.

Borders

Rnd 5 Border: With right side facing, join Color B with sc in any sc of Rnd 5; *ch 3, sc in top of each of next 7 dc, ch 3, sc in next sc; rep from * around, ending last rep with join, finish off.

Rnd 3 Border: With right side facing, join Color B with sc in any sc of Rnd 3; *ch 3, sc each of next 5 dc, ch 3, sc in next sc; rep from * around, ending last rep with join. Finish off; weave in yarn ends.

Pansy

Bottom Petals: Join Color C with sc in next ch-6 lp; in same lp work (hdc, 6 dc, hdc, sc); in next ch-7 lp work (sc, hdc, 7 dc, hdc, sc); in next ch-6 lp work (sc, hdc, 6 dc, hdc, sc). Finish off Color C; weave in yarn ends.

Three colors:
Color A (yellow)
Color B (purple)
Color C (lavender)

Instructions

Rnd 1: With Color A, ch 2, work 5 sc in 2nd ch from hook. Finish off Color A.

Rnd 2: Join Color B with sl st in any sc; (ch 8, sl st in next sc) twice; ch 6, sl st in next sc, ch 7, sl st in next sc, ch 6; join with sc in beg ch-8 lp.

Top Petals: In same ch-8 lp work [hdc, dc, tr, (ch 1, tr) 9 times, dc, hdc, sc]; in next ch-8 lp work [sc, hdc, dc, tr, (ch 1, tr) 9 times, dc, hdc, sc]. Finish off Color B.

Petite Floral

Instructions
Ch 4, join with sl st to form a ring.

Rnd 1: Ch 1, work 12 sc in ring; join with sl st in beg sc.

Rnd 2: *Ch 4, sl st in next sc; rep from * around, end last rep with sl st in beg sl st. Finish off; weave in yarn ends.

Dainty Daffy

Instructions

Ch 2.

Rnd 1: In 2nd ch from hook work 6 sc; join with sl st in back lp only of beg sc.

Rnd 2: Ch 3 **(counts as first dc of rnd)**; working in back lp only of each st, (2 dc in next sc, dc in next sc) twice, 2 dc in last sc; join in top of beg ch-3: 9 dc. Finish off.

Rnd 3: Join yarn with sl st in any unused lp of Rnd 1; ch 1, 2 sc in same lp; work 2 sc in each rem lp around: 12 sc; join with sl st in beg sc.

Rnd 4: Ch 4; work (2 tr, ch 4, sl st) in same sc as joining, sl st in next sc; *in next sc work (sl st, ch 4, 2 tr, ch 4, sl st), sl st in next sc; rep from *around: 6 petals made; join. Finish off; weave in yarn ends.

Wavy Petals

Two colors:
Color A (gold)
Color B (deep pink)

Instructions

With Color A, ch 5, join with sl st to form a ring.

Rnd 1: Sl st in ring; ch 6 (counts as a tr and ch-2 sp), tr in ring; (ch 2, tr in ring) 10 times, ch 2; join with sc in 4th ch of beg ch-6: 12 tr and 12 ch-2 sps.

Rnd 2: * Work 2 sc in next ch-2 sp, sc in next tr; rep from * around, ending last rep with 2 sc in last ch-2 sp: 36 sc; join with sc in beg sc.

Rnd 3: *Ch 3, skip next sc, sc in next sc; rep from * around, ending last rep with join with sl st in beg sc: 18 ch-3 sps. Finish off Color A.

Rnd 4: Join Color B in any ch-3 sp; ch 3 (counts as a dc), work 7 dc in same sp; *work 8 dc in next ch-3 sp; rep from * around; join with sc in 3rd ch of beg ch-3.

Rnd 5: *Ch 2, skip next dc, sc in next dc; rep from * around, ending last rep with sl st in joining sc. Finish off; weave in yarn ends.

Rosy Posies

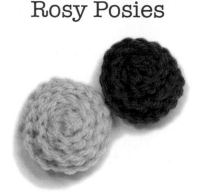

Note: *The size of these rolled roses is determined by the length of the foundation chain. The chain for the smaller rose is given first, with the chain for the larger in parentheses.*

Instructions
Ch 15 (20).

Row 1: Work 2 dc in 2nd ch from hook; *3 dc in next ch; rep from * across; finish off, leaving a 6" (15 cm) yarn end.

Starting at beg of row, roll the row on itself, with the first sts made forming the center. Thread yarn end into a tapestry needle and stitch last dc to rest of rose. Take several stitches completely through the rose to hold the roll in place.

Puffy Petals

Rnd 2: *Ch 2, skip next sc, sc in next sc; rep from * around, ending last rep with ch 2; join in beg sc: 6 ch-2 sps. Finish off Color A.

Rnd 3: Join Color B with sl st in any ch-2 sp; in same sp work (ch 3, PC, ch 3, sl st); *in next ch-2 sp work (sl st, ch 3, PC, ch 3, sl st); rep from * around; join. Finish off Color B; weave in yarn ends.

Two colors:
Color A (dk pink)
Color B (yellow)

Stitch Guide

Popcorn Stitch (PC): Work 4 dc in specified sp; drop lp from hook, insert hook from front to back in top of first dc made, pick up dropped lp and draw through: PC made.

Instructions

With Color A, ch 6, join with sl st to form a ring.

Rnd 1: Ch 1, work 12 sc in ring; join with sc in first sc.

Sunny Flower

Two colors:
Color A (orange)
Color B (gold)

Instructions

With Color A, ch 4.

Rnd 1: Work 11 dc in 4th ch from hook; join with sl st in top of beg ch.

Rnd 2: Ch 3 (counts as first dc of rnd), dc in joining; work 2 dc in each st around; join with sl st in top of beg ch: 24 dc. Finish off Color A.

Rnd 3: Join Color B with sc in any dc; *ch 20, sc in next dc; rep from * around, ending last rep with sl st in beg sc. Finish off; weave in yarn ends.

Bluette

Three colors:
Color A (gold)
Color B (med blue)
Color C (lt blue)

Instructions

With Color A, ch 4, join with sl st to form a ring.

Rnd 1: Sl st in ring; ch 4 (equals a dc and ch-1 sp), (dc in ring, ch 1) 7 times; join in 3rd ch of beg ch-4: 8 ch-1 sps. Finish off Color A.

Rnd 2: Join Color B in any ch-1 sp; ch 3, dc in same sp; *ch 2, 2 dc in next ch-1 sp; rep from * around, ending last rep with ch 2; join in top of beg ch-3.

Rnd 3: Sl st in next dc and into next ch-2 sp; in same sp work (sc, ch 6, sc), ch 3; *in next ch-2 sp work (sc, ch 6, sc), ch 3; rep from * around; join in beg sc. Finish off Color B.

Rnd 4: Join Color C with sc in any ch-3 sp; *work 12 dc in next ch-6 sp, sc in next ch-3 sp; rep from * around, ending last rep with join in beg sc. Finish off Color C; weave in yarn ends.

Tipped Petals

Two colors:
Color A (yellow)
Color B (pink)

Stitch Guide

Popcorn (PC): Work 4 dc in ring; drop lp from hook, insert hook from front to back in top of first dc worked, insert hook in dropped lp and draw through, ch 1: PC made.

Instructions

With Color A, ch 8; join with sl st to form a ring.

Rnd 1: Sl st in ring, ch 3; (work PC in ring, ch 2) 8 times; join in top of beg PC. Finish off Color A.

Rnd 2: Join Color B with sl st in any ch-2 sp; *ch 8, sl st in 2nd ch from hook, sc in next ch, hdc in next ch, dc in each of next 3 chs, hdc in last ch, sl st in next ch-2 sp; rep from * around, ending last rep with join in beg sl st. Finish off; weave in yarn ends.

Bold Bloom

Two Colors:

Color A (lime green)

Color B (bright pink)

Stitch Guide

Cluster (CL): *YO, insert hook in ring and draw up a lp to height of a dc, YO and draw through 2 lps; rep from * 3 times more, YO and draw through 5 lps: CL made.

Instructions

With Color A, ch 8, join with sl st to form a ring.

Rnd 1 (right side): Ch 3; *work CL in ring, ch 3; rep from * 7 times more; join with sl st in top of first CL: 8 ch-3 sps; finish off Color A.

Rnd 2: Join Color B with sc in any ch-3 sp between CLs; in same sp work (hdc, 2 dc, tr, 2 dc, hdc, sc): petal made; *in next ch-3 sp between CLs work petal of (sc, hdc, 2 dc, tr, 2 dc, hdc, sc); rep from * around; join in beg sc: 8 petals made.

Rnd 3: Ch 2; turn piece to wrong side; *sc in back strands of next sc to right, ch 3, sc in back strands of next tr, ch 3; rep from * around; join: 16 ch-3 sps.

Rnd 4: Turn piece to right side; in each ch-3 sp work petal of (sc, hdc, dc, tr, dc, hdc, sc): 16 petals made; join. Finish off, weave in yarn ends.

Fanciful Flower

Four colors:
Color A (lime green)
Color B (yellow)
Color C (purple)
Color D (lavender)

Instructions

Rnd 1: With Color A, ch 5 (counts as a dc and ch-1 sp); in 5th ch from hook work (dc, ch 1) 5 times; join in 4th ch of beg ch-5: 6 ch-1 sps. Finish off Color A.

Rnd 2: Join Color B with sc in any ch-1 sp, in same sp work (hdc, 2 dc, hdc, sc): petal made; *in next ch-1 sp work petal of (sc, hdc, 2 dc, hdc, sc); rep from * around; join with sl st in beg sc. Finish off Color B.

Rnd 3: Working behind petals of Rnd 2, join Color C with sl st in strands at back of center 2 dc sts of any petal; *ch 4; join with sl st in strands at back of center 2 dc sts of next petal; rep from * around, ending last rep with ch 4; join with sl st in beg sl st: 6 ch-4 sps.

Rnd 4: *In next ch-4 sp work petal of (sc, hdc, 4 dc, hdc, sc); rep from * around; join with sl st in beg sc. Finish off Color C.

Rnd 5: Working behind petals of Rnd 4, join Color D with sl st in strands at back of center 2 dc of any petal; *ch 5, sl st in strands at back of center 2 dc of next petal; rep from * around, ending last rep with sl st in beg sl st.

Rnd 6: *In next ch-5 sp work petal of (sc, hdc, 2 dc, 2 tr, 2 dc, hdc, sc); rep from * around; join with sl st in beg sc. Finish off Color D; weave in yarn ends.

Irish Crochet Rose

Stitch Guide

Front Post Single Crochet (FPsc): Insert hook from front to back to front around post (vertical bar) of specified st and draw up a lp, YO and draw through both lps on hook: FPsc made.

Instructions

Ch 8, join with sl st to form a ring.

Rnd 1: Ch 1, work 16 sc in ring; join in beg sc.

Rnd 2: Ch 6 (counts as a dc and ch-3 sp), skip next sc, dc in next sc, (ch 3, skip next sc, dc in next sc) 6 times, ch 3, skip next sc; join in 3rd ch of beg ch-6: 8 ch-3 lps.

Rnd 3: *In next ch-3 sp work (sc, hdc, 3 dc, hdc, sc): petal made; rep from * around: 8 petals made; join in beg sc. Finish off.

Rnd 4: Working behind petals of Rnd 3, join yarn with FPsc around any dc of Rnd 2; *ch 4, FPsc around next dc; rep from * around, ending last rep with ch 4; join in beg sc: 8 ch-4 lps.

Rnd 5: *In next ch-4 lp work petal of (sc, hdc, 4 dc, hdc, sc); rep from * around; join with sl st in beg sc. Finish off.

LEAVES

Leaf 1

Instructions

Ch 10.

Rnd 1: Sc in 2nd ch from hook, hdc in each of next 2 chs, dc in each of next 5 chs, 10 tr in last ch; working now in unused lps on opposite side of ch, dc in each of next 5 lps, hdc in each of next 2 lps, sc in last lp; join with sl st in beg sc. Ch 4 for stem, sl st in 2nd ch from hook and in next 2 chs; join with sl st in first st of rnd. Finish off; weave in yarn ends.

Leaf 2

Instructions

Ch 8.

Rnd 1: Sc in 2nd ch from hook, hdc in next ch, dc in each of next 4 chs, work 10 tr in next ch; working now in unused lps on opposite side of ch, dc in each of next 4 lps, hdc in next 2 lps; join with sl st in beg sc. Ch 4 for stem, sl st in 2nd ch from hook and in next 2 chs; join with sl st in first st of rnd. Finish off; weave in yarn ends.

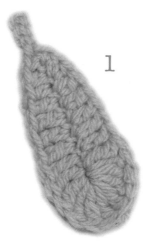

1

2

Leaf 3

Instructions

Ch 18.

Rnd 1: Sl st in 2nd ch from hook, sc in next 2 chs, hdc in next 2 chs, dc in next 2 chs, 2 dc in next ch, tr in next 2 chs, dc in next 2 chs, hdc in next 2 chs, sc in next 2 chs, in next ch work (sc, ch 1, sc); working now on opposite side of ch in unused lps, sc in next 2 chs, hdc in next 2 chs, dc in next 2 chs, tr in next 2 chs, 2 dc in next ch; dc in next 2 chs, hdc in next 2 chs, sc in next 2 chs; sl st in next ch; join with sl st in beg sl st.

Rnd 2: Sl st in back lp of first st, sc in back lp of each st along first side of ch to ch-1 sp, work 3 sc in ch-1 sp; sc in back lp of each st along opposite side of ch to last st, sl st in back lp of last st; join. Finish off; weave in yarn ends.

Leaf 4

Instructions

Ch 10.

Row 1: Sl st in 2nd ch from hook and in next ch; sc in next 2 chs, dc in next 2 chs, 3 dc in next ch; hdc in next ch, sc in last ch. Finish off; weave in yarn ends.

3

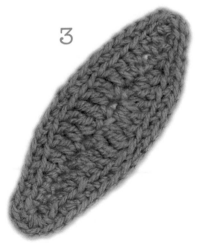

4

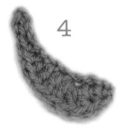

Leaf 5

Instructions

Ch 8, join with sl st to form a ring.

Rnd 1: In ring work (sc, 2 hdc, 6 dc, 2 tr, 6 dc, 2 hdc, sc); ch 7 for stem, sl st in 2nd ch from hook and in next 5 chs; join with sl st in beg sc. Finish off; weave in yarn ends.

Leaf 6

Instructions

Ch 6, join with sl st to form a ring.

Rnd 1: In ring work sc, 2 hdc, 5 dc, tr, 5 dc, 2 hdc, sc; ch 5 for stem, sl st in 2nd ch from hook and in next 3 chs; join with sl st in beg sc. Finish off; weave in yarn ends.

Leaf 7

Instructions

Ch 4.

Rnd 1: Work 11 dc in 4th ch from hook; join with sl st in top of beg ch-4.

Rnd 2: Ch 3, dc in joining; 2 dc in each dc around: 24 dc; join in 3rd ch of beg ch-3; ch 5 for stem, sl st in 2nd ch from hook and in next 3 chs; join. Finish off, weave in yarn ends.

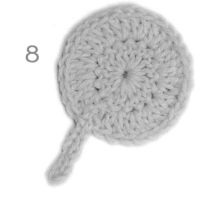

Leaf 8

Instructions

Ch 4.

Rnd 1: Work 15 dc in 4th ch from hook; join with sl st in top of beg ch-4.

Rnd 2: Ch 3, dc in joining; 2 dc in each dc around: 32 dc; join in 3rd ch of beg ch-3; ch 8 for stem, sl st in 2nd ch from hook and in next 6 chs; join. Finish off; weave in yarn ends.

Leaf 9

Instructions

Ch 4, join with sl st to form a ring.

Row 1: Sl st into ring, ch 3, work 5 dc in ring; do not join; ch 3, turn.

Row 2: Dc in base of ch; 2 dc in each rem dc; ch 1, turn.

Row 3: Sc in first dc, *ch 2; sc in next dc; rep from * across, ending with ch 2, sc in 3rd ch of turning ch. Finish off; weave in yarn ends.

Leaf 10

Instructions

Ch 6, join with sl st to form a ring.

Row 1: Sl st into ring, ch 3, work 8 dc in ring; do not join; ch 3, turn.

Row 2: Dc in base of ch; 2 dc in each rem dc; ch 1, turn.

Row 3: Sc in first dc; *ch 2, sc in next dc; rep from * across, ending with ch 2, sc in 3rd ch of turning ch. Finish off; weave in yarn ends.

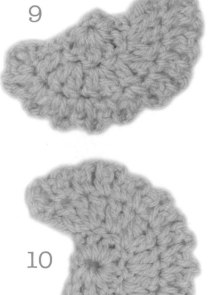

9

10

Leaf 11

Instructions

Ch 5.

Row 1: Sl st in 2nd ch from hook and in next 3 chs; ch 3 (counts as a dc on following row).

Row 2: Work 11 dc in base of ch; ch 4 (counts as a dc and ch-1 sp on following row), turn.

Row 3: *Dc in next dc, ch 1; rep from * across, ending last rep with dc in last dc; ch 1, turn.

Row 4: Sc in first dc; *ch 2, sc in next dc; rep from * across. Finish off; weave in yarn ends.

Leaf 12

Instructions

Ch 11.

Rnd 1: Sc in 2nd ch from hook and in next ch; hdc in next ch, dc in each of next 4 chs, hdc in next ch, sc in next ch, work 3 sc in last ch; working now in unused lps on opposite side of foundation ch, sc in next lp, hdc in next lp, dc in each of next 4 lps, hdc in next lp, sc in each of last 2 lps; join with sl st in beg sc.

Rnd 2: *Ch 1, sc in next st; rep from * around; join. Finish off; weave in yarn ends.

11

12

Leaf 13

Instructions

Ch 2.

Row 1: Work 3 sc in 2nd ch from hook; ch 1, turn.

Row 2: Work 2 sc in first sc, sc in next sc, 2 sc in last sc: 5 sc; ch 1, turn.

Row 3: Work 2 sc in first sc, sc in next 3 sc, 2 sc in last sc: 7 sc; ch 1, turn.

Rows 4 through 9: Sc in each sc; ch 1, turn.

Row 10: Draw up a lp in each of first 2 sc, YO and draw through 3 lps: dec made; sc in each sc to last 2 sc, draw up a lp in each of next 2 sc, YO and draw through 3 lps: dec made: 5 sc; ch 1, turn.

Row 11: Rep Row 10: 3 sc; ch 1, turn.

Row 12: Draw up a lp in each rem sc, YO and draw through 4 lps. Finish off; weave in yarn ends.

13

BORDERS

Crocheted borders add a finishing touch
to afghans, clothing or household items
and make a nice change from fringe.

At the beginning of each border pattern
is a multiple, like this: Chain multiple: 6 + 3. The
multiple refers to the number of foundation chains
you need to complete one unit of the pattern. The
number following the + sign shows the extra chains
needed for the pattern to begin and end correctly.

For example, if the chain multiple is 6 + 3, you can
make a chain with any multiple of 6: 12, 18, 24 and so
on, then add the +3. The "+" number is added just once.

Borders can be applied to the final edge of a
project, or they can be worked directly on the
last row of the project.

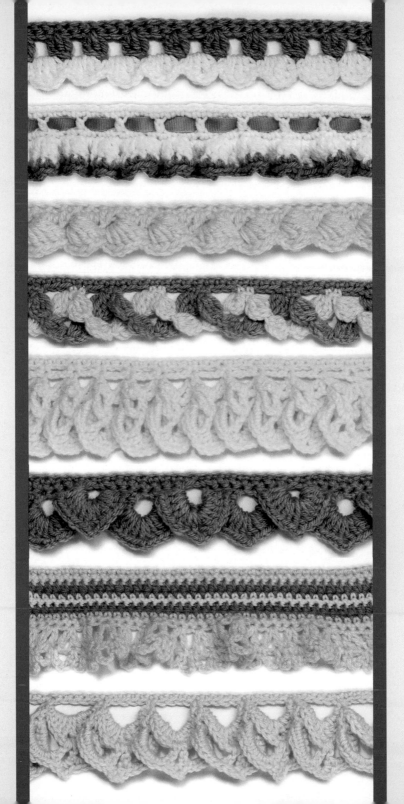

Cluster Shells

Chain multiple: 3 + 2

Two colors:
Color A (lavender)
Color B (off white)

Stitch Guide

Cluster (CL): *YO, insert hook in specified st and draw up a lp, YO and draw through 2 lps; rep from * in same st 2 times more, YO and draw through 4 lps: CL made.

Instructions

Work foundation chain with Color A.

Row 1: With Color A, sc in 2nd ch from hook and in each rem ch; ch 5 (counts as a dc and ch-2 sp on following row), turn.

Row 2 (right side): Skip next 2 sc, CL in next sc; *ch 2, skip next 2 sc, CL in next sc; rep from * to last 3 sc, ch 2, skip next 2 sc, dc in last sc. Finish off Color A.

Row 3: Hold piece with right side facing; join Color B with sc in 3rd ch of turning ch-5; in rem ch sp of same turning ch work (sc, dc, tr, dc, sc), sc in next CL; *in next ch-2 sp work (sc, dc, tr, dc, sc)**, sc in next CL; rep from * across, ending last rep at **; sc in last dc. Finish off; weave in yarn ends.

Ruffles and Ribbons

Chain multiple: 2

Two colors:
Color A (white)
Color B (lavender)

Additional Materials:
Ribbon of desired length.

Instructions
Work foundation chain with Color A.

Row 1: With Color A, sc in 2nd ch from hook and in each rem ch; ch 4 (counts as a dc and ch-1 sp on following row), turn.

Row 2 (right side): *Skip next sc, dc in next sc, ch 1; rep from * across, ending last rep with dc in last sc. Finish off Color A.

Row 3 (right side): Hold piece with right side facing; join Color A with sc in 3rd ch of turning ch-4; *sc in next ch-1 sp, sc in next dc; rep from * across. Finish off Color A.

Row 4 (right side): With right side facing and starting ch at top, working in unused lps of foundation ch, join Color A with sl st in first lp at right, ch 3, dc in same lp; *ch 1, 2 dc in next unused lp; rep from * across. Finish off.

Row 5 (right side): Hold piece with right side facing and Row 4 at top. Join Color B with sc in 3rd ch of beg ch-3 on Row 4; sc in each dc and in each ch-1 sp across. Finish off; weave in yarn ends.

Finishing
Weave ribbon through mesh formed in Row 2. Sew ribbon ends securely in place.

Slanting Shells

Chain multiple: 3 + 2

Stitch Guide

Front Post Double Crochet (FPdc): YO; insert hook around post (vertical bar) of specified st from front to back to front and draw up a lp to height of a dc; YO and draw through 2 lps twice: FPdc made.

Instructions

Row 1 (right side): Sc in 2nd ch from hook and in each rem ch; ch 3 (counts as first dc on following row), turn.

Row 2: Dc in next sc and in each rem sc across; ch 1, turn.

Row 3: Sc in first dc; *sc in next dc, work 5 FPdc around post of same dc, dc in next 2 dc; rep from * across to last 2 sts, dc in next dc, sc in 3rd ch of turning ch-3. Finish off; weave in yarn ends.

Over and Under

Chain multiple: 8 + 2

Two colors:
Color A (med green)
Color B (lt green)

Stitch Guide

Cluster (CL): *YO, insert hook in specified ch and draw up a lp to height of a dc, YO and draw through 2 lps on hook; rep from * in same ch 2 times more, YO and draw through all 4 lps on hook: CL made.

Instructions

Work foundation chain with Color A.

Row 1 (right side): With Color A, sc in 2nd ch from hook and in each rem ch. Finish off.

Row 2 (right side): With right side facing, join Color A with sc in first sc at right on Row 1; (ch 4, CL in 4th ch from hook) 4 times, skip next 6 sc, sc in next 2 sc; leaving a long lp, remove hook from lp and drop Color A to front of work; working in front of Color A CLs, skip first 2 sc on Row 1, join Color B with sc in next sc, sc in next sc; (ch 4, CL in 4th ch from hook) 4 times; skip next 2 sc after last 2 sc worked in Color A, sc in next 2 sc; *leaving a long lp, remove hook from lp and drop Color B to front of work; **return dropped lp of Color A to hook, working with Color A in front of CLs Color B, (ch 4, CL in 4th ch from hook) 4 times, skip next 2 sc after last 2 sc worked in Color B, sc in next 2 sc***; leaving a long lp, remove hook from lp and drop Color A to front of work; return dropped lp of Color B to hook; working with Color B in front of CLs of Color A, (ch 4, CL in 4th ch from hook) 4 times, skip next 2 sc after last 2 sc worked in Color A, sc in next 2 sc; rep from * across to last 4 sc. Finish off Color B; rep from ** to *** once. Finish off Color A; weave in yarn ends.

Elegance

Chain multiple: 3 + 2

Instructions

Row 1 (right side): Sc in 2nd ch from hook and in each rem ch; ch 1, turn.

Row 2: Sc in first sc; *ch 3, skip 2 sc, sc in next sc; rep from * across; ch 1, turn.

Row 3: Sc in first sc; *ch 5, sc in next sc; rep from * across; ch 1, turn.

Row 4: Sc in first sc; *ch 7, sc in next sc; rep from * across; ch 1, turn.

Row 5: Sc in first sc; ch 5, dc in front of ch-7 lp of Row 3 and over ch-5 lp of Row 2; ch 5, sc in next sc; *ch 5, dc in front of next ch-7 and over ch-5 lp as before, ch 5, sc in next sc; rep from * across; ch 1, turn.

Row 6: Sc in first sc; *ch 5, (dc, ch 3, dc) in next dc; ch 5, sc in next sc; rep from * across; ch 1, turn.

Row 7: *Work 5 sc in next ch-5 lp, (2 dc, ch 3, 2 dc) in next ch-3 lp; 5 sc in next ch-5 lp, sc in next sc; rep from * across. Finish off; weave in yarn ends.

Pointed Shells

Chain multiple: 8 + 3

Stitch Guide

Shell: Work (7 dc, ch 3, 7 dc) in specified lp: shell made.

Instructions

Row 1 (right side): Sc in 2nd ch from hook and in each rem ch; ch 1, turn.

Row 2: Sc in first 5 sc; *ch 5, sc in next 8 sc; rep from * across to last 5 sc; ch 5, sc in last 5 sc; ch 1, turn.

Row 3: Sc in first sc, ch 5, sc in next sc; *shell in next ch-5 lp, skip next 3 sc, sc in next sc, ch 5, sc in next sc; rep from * across; finish off.

Row 4 (right side): With right side facing, join yarn with sl st in first ch-5 lp at right, ch 3 (counts as dc), 7 dc in same ch-5 lp; *ch 1; working behind next shell, sl st in back lps at bottom of center 2 dc *(see fig)*, ch 1; work shell in next ch-5 lp; rep from * across, ending last rep with 7 dc in last ch-5 lp, ch 3, sl st in same lp. Finish off; weave in yarn ends.

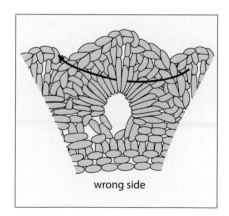

wrong side

Pastel Parade

Chain multiple: Any even number

Three colors:
Color A (lt pink)
Color B (hot pink)
Color C (lime green)

Instructions

Work foundation chain with Color A.

Row 1 (right side): With Color A, sc in 2nd ch from hook and in each rem ch; ch 1, turn.

Row 2: Sc in each sc across, changing to Color B in last st; with Color B, ch 2 (counts as first hdc on following row), turn. Finish off Color A.

Row 3: With Color B, hdc next sc and in each rem sc. At end of row, finish off Color B.

Row 4: Hold piece with right side facing; join Color C with sc in top of ch-2 at right; sc in each hdc across, ch 1, turn.

Row 5: Sc in each sc across; at end of row, change to Color B in last st; ch 2 (counts as first hdc on following row), turn. Finish off Color C.

Row 6: With Color B, hdc in next sc and in each rem sc; at end of row, finish off Color B.

Row 7: Hold piece with right side facing; join Color A with sc in top of ch-2 at right; sc in each sc across; ch 1, turn.

Row 8: Sc in each sc across, ch 5 (counts as a dc and ch-2 sp on following row), turn.

Row 9: Dc in first sc; *skip next sc, work (dc, ch 2, dc) in next sc; rep from across; ch 1, turn.

Row 10: Sc in first dc; *ch 4, sc in next dc; rep from * across. Finish off; weave in all yarn ends.

Fancy Shells

Chain multiple: 5 + 2

Stitch Guide

Shell: In specified lp work (sc, hdc, 2 dc, tr, ch 3, tr, 2 dc, hdc, sc): shell made.

Instructions

Row 1 (right side): Sc in 2nd ch from hook and in each rem ch; ch 1, turn.

Row 2: Sc in first sc; *ch 8, skip 4 sc, sc in next sc; rep from * across; ch 1, turn.

Row 3: Sc in first sc; *work shell in next ch-8 lp, sc in next sc; rep from * across; ch 1, turn.

Row 4: Sc in first sc; *ch 6, in next ch-3 sp of next shell work (dc, ch 3, dc); ch 6, sc in next sc; rep from * across; ch 1, turn.

Row 5: Sc in first sc; * work 8 sc in next ch-6 sp, (sc, ch 3, sc) in next ch-3 sp; work 8 sc in next ch-6 sp, sc in next sc; rep from * across. Finish off; weave in yarn ends.

BANDS

Bands are similar to borders, but have a decorative edge on both top and bottom, rather than on just the bottom as in borders. They are wonderful accents for clothing and towels, or as a shelf accent.

At the beginning of each band pattern is a multiple, like this: Chain multiple: 6 + 3. The multiple refers to the number of foundation chains you need to complete one unit of the pattern. The number following the + sign shows the extra chains needed for the pattern to begin and end correctly.

For example, if the chain multiple is 6 + 3, you can make a chain with any multiple of 6: 12, 18, 24, and so on, then add the +3. The "+" number is added just once.

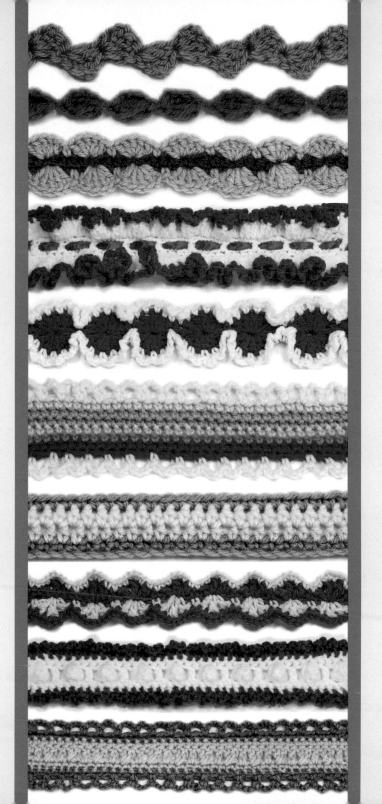

Rickrack

Note: *Pattern is not worked on a foundation chain base.*

Instructions

Ch 4.

Row 1: Work 3 dc in 4th ch from hook; ch 3, turn.

Row 2: Work 3 dc in first dc; ch 3, turn, leaving rem dc unworked.

Repeat Row 2 for desired length. Finish off; weave in yarn ends.

Linked Clusters

Note: *Pattern is not worked on a foundation chain base.*

Stitch Guide

Cluster (CL): *YO, insert hook in 4th ch from hook and draw up a lp to height of a dc; YO and draw through 2 lps; rep from * 2 times more in same ch, YO and draw through 4 lps: CL made.

Instructions

Row 1: *Ch 4, work CL in 4th ch from hook; rep from * for desired length of band. Finish off; weave in yarn ends.

Lilac Shells

Chain multiple: 4 + 2

Two colors:
Color A (purple)
Color B (lilac)

Stitch Guide

Shell: Work 5 dc in specified st: shell made.

Instructions

Work foundation chain with Color A.

Row 1 (right side): With Color A, sc in 2nd ch from hook and in each rem ch. Finish off Color A.

Row 2 (right side): With right side facing, join Color B with sc in first sc at right; *skip next sc, shell in next sc, skip next sc, sc in next sc; rep from * across. Finish off Color B.

Row 3 (right side): With right side facing, turn work so foundation ch is at top. Working in unused lps of foundation ch, join Color B with sc in first lp at right; *skip next lp, shell in next lp, skip next lp, sc in next lp; rep from * across. Finish off; weave in yarn ends.

Scarlet Ribbons

Chain multiple: Any even number

Two colors:
Color A (white)
Color B (red)

Additional Materials:
Ribbon of desired length.

Note: *Row 2 can be adjusted to fit various sizes of ribbon. For wider ribbon, work Row 2 with dc or tr instead of hdc. If working Row 2 with dc, ch 1 more at end of Row 1; if working Row 2 with tr, ch 2 more at end of Row 1.*

Instructions
Work foundation chain with Color A.

Row 1 (right side): With Color A, sc in 2nd ch from hook and in each rem ch; ch 3 (counts as hdc and ch-1 sp on following row), turn.

Row 2: Skip next sc; *hdc in next sc, ch 1, sk next sc; rep from * across, ending last rep with hdc in last sc; ch 1, turn.

Row 3: Sc in first hdc; sc in each ch-1 sp and in each hdc across, ending last rep with sc in turning ch-3 sp, sc in 2nd ch of turning ch-3. Finish off Color A.

Row 4 (right side): With right side facing, join Color A with sl st in first sc at right; ch 3, work 2 dc in base of ch; *work 2 dc in next sc, 3 dc in next sc; rep from * across. Finish off Color A.

Row 5 (right side): With right side facing, join Color B with sc in 3rd ch of beg ch-3 on Row 4; *ch 1, sc in next dc; rep from * across. Finish off Color B.

Row 6 (right side): Hold piece with right side facing and foundation chain at top. Working in unused lps of foundation ch, join Color A with sl st in first lp at right; ch 3, work 2 dc in base of ch-3; *work 2 dc in next lp, work 3 dc in next lp; rep from * across. Finish off Color A.

Row 7 (right side): With right side facing, join Color B with sc in top of turning ch at right of Row 6; *ch 1, sc in next dc; rep from * across. Finish off Color B; weave in yarn ends.

Finishing
Weave ribbon through mesh formed in Row 2. Sew ribbon ends securely in place.

Ruffled Row

Chain multiple: 4 + 2

Two colors:
Color A (red)
Color B (white)

Stitch Guide
Shell: Work 5 dc in specified st: shell made.

Instructions
Work foundation chain with Color A.

Row 1 (right side): With Color A, sc in 2nd ch from hook; *skip next ch, shell in next ch, skip next ch, sc in next ch; rep from * across. Finish off Color A.

Row 2 (right side): With right side facing, join Color B with sc in first sc at right; *(ch 3, sc in next dc of shell) 5 times, ch 3, sc in next sc; rep from * across. Finish off Color B.

Row 3 (right side): Hold piece with right side facing and foundation ch at top. Working in unused lps of foundation ch, join Color A with sc in first lp at right, skip next lp, shell in next lp (same ch in which shell was worked on Row 1), skip next lp, sc in next lp; rep from * across. Finish off Color A.

Row 4 (right side): With right side facing, join Color B with sc in first sc at right of Row 3; *(ch 3, sc in next dc of shell) 5 times, ch 3, sc in next sc; rep from * across. Finish off Color B. Weave in yarn ends.

Rainbow

Chain multiple: Any even number

Seven colors:
Color A (red)
Color B (orange)
Color C (bright yellow)
Color D (green)
Color E (blue)
Color F (lavender)
Color G (pale yellow)

Instructions
Work foundation chain with Color A.

Row 1 (right side): Sc in 2nd ch from hook and in each rem ch. Finish off Color A.

Row 2 (right side): Hold piece with right side facing; join Color B with sc in first sc at right; sc in each sc across. Finish off Color B.

Rnds 3 through 6: Rep Row 2 four times more, once each with Color C, Color D, Color E and Color F, in that order.

Top Border: Hold piece with right side facing and last row worked at top. Join Color G with sc in first sc at right; *ch 3, skip next sc, sc in next sc; rep from * across. Finish off.

Bottom Border: Hold piece with right side facing and foundation chain at top. Working in unused lps of foundation ch, join Color G with sc in first ch at right; *ch 3, skip next ch, sc in next ch; rep from * across. Finish off; weave in yarn ends.

Tri-Color Ribbon

Chain multiple: Any number

Three colors:
Color A (green)
Color B (pink)
Color C (yellow)

Instructions
Work foundation chain with Color A.

Row 1 (right side): With Color A, sc in 2nd ch from hook and in each rem ch, changing to Color B in last st; with Color B, ch 1, turn. Finish off Color A.

Row 2: With Color B, sc in first sc and in each sc across, changing to Color C in last st; with Color C, ch 1, turn. Finish off Color B.

Row 3: With Color C, sc in first sc and in each sc across, changing to Color A in last st; with Color A, ch 1, turn.

Row 4: With Color A, sc in first sc and in each sc across. Finish off Color A; weave in yarn ends.

Topsy Turvy

Chain multiple: 4 + 2

Two colors:
Color A (rose)
Color B (pink)

Stitch Guide
Shell: In specified st work (dc, ch 1) twice, dc in same st: shell made.

Instructions
Work foundation chain with Color A.

Row 1 (right side): With Color A, sc in 2nd ch from hook; *skip next ch, work shell in next ch, skip next ch, sc in next ch; rep from * across. Finish off Color A.

Row 2 (right side): With right side facing, join Color B with sc in first sc at right; *sc in first dc of next shell, sc in next ch-1 sp, work 3 sc in next dc, sc in next ch-1 sp, sc in next dc, sc in next sc; rep from * across. Finish off Color B.

Row 3 (right side): With right side facing, hold piece with foundation ch at top; working in unused lps of foundation ch, join Color B with sc in first lp at right; *skip next lp, work shell in next lp (same ch in which shell was previously worked on Row 1), skip next lp, sc in next lp; rep from * across. Finish off Color B.

Row 4 (right side): With right side facing, join Color A with sc in first sc at right; *sc in first dc of next shell, sc in next ch-1 sp, work 3 sc in next dc, sc in ch-1 sp, sc in next dc, sc in next sc; rep from * across. Finish off Color A; weave in yarn ends.

Snow Balls

Chain multiple: 4 + 2

Two colors:
Color A (white)
Color B (blue)

Stitch Guide

Popcorn Stitch (PC): Work 4 dc in specified st. Drop lp from hook, insert hook from front to back in top of first dc worked; insert hook in dropped lp and draw through, ch 1 to tighten st (PC made).
Note: *Final ch 1 of PC does not count as a ch-1 sp on row following.*

Instructions
Work foundation chain with Color A.

Row 1: With Color A, sc in 2nd ch from hook and in each rem ch; ch 4 (counts as a dc and ch-1 sp on following row), turn.

Row 2 (right side): *Skip next sc, PC in next sc, ch 1 (in addition to final ch-1 of PC), skip next sc, dc in next sc **, ch 1; rep from * across, ending last rep at **; ch 1, turn.

Row 3: Sc in first dc; *sc in next ch-1 sp, sc in next PC **, sc in next ch-1 sp, sc in next dc; rep from * across, ending last rep at **, sc in turning ch-4 sp, sc in 3rd ch of turning ch-4. Finish off Color A.

Row 4: Hold piece with right side facing and Row 3 at top; join Color B with sc in first sc at right; *ch 3, sc in next sc; rep from * across. Finish off Color B.

Row 5: Hold piece with right side facing and foundation ch at top; working in unused lps of foundation ch, join Color B with sc in first lp at right; *ch 3, sc in next lp; rep from * across. Finish off; weave in yarn ends.

Crossed Stitches

Chain multiple: 6 + 2

Two colors:
Color A (lt blue)
Color B (med blue)

Instructions
Work foundation chain with Color A.

Row 1 (right side): With Color A, sc in 2nd ch from hook and in each rem ch; ch 3 (counts as a dc on following row), turn.

Row 2: *Skip next sc, dc in next sc, dc in skipped sc, dc in next sc; rep from * across; ch 1, turn.

Row 3: Sc in first dc and in each dc across. Finish off Color A.

Row 4: With right side facing, join Color B with sc in first sc at right of Row 3; sc in first sc and in each sc across, ch 1, turn.

Row 5: Sc in first sc; *ch 3, skip next sc, sc in next sc; rep from * across. Finish off.

Row 6: Hold piece with right side facing and foundation ch at top. Working in unused lps of foundation ch, join Color B with sc in first lp at right; sc in next lp and in each lp across, ch 1, turn.

Row 7: Sc in first sc; *ch 3, skip next sc, sc in next sc; rep from * across. Finish off; weave in yarn ends.

BRAIDS

This collection of braids is truly international: it includes braids from Russia, the Ukraine, Belgium, and Romania. Several of these braids are traditionally used in ethnic laces. Braids are quick and easy to make. We've shown ours worked in size 3 crochet cotton, but they can be crocheted in any weight yarn you prefer. Smooth yarns make the braid details stand out.

Braid 1

Instructions

Ch 10.

Row 1: Dc in 6th ch from hook and in each rem ch across: 5 dc; ch 5, turn.

Row 2: Dc in each dc; ch 5, turn.

Repeat Row 2 for pattern. At end of last row, do not ch or turn. Finish off.

Braid 2

Instructions

Ch 2.

Row 1: Work 3 sc in 2nd ch from hook: 3 sc; ch 1, turn.

Row 2: Sc in first sc, 2 sc in front lp of next sc: 3 sc; ch 1, turn, leaving rem sc unworked.

Repeat Row 2 until braid is desired length. At end of last row, do not ch or turn. Finish off.

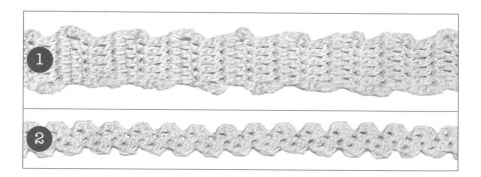

Braid 3

Instructions

Ch 3.

Row 1: Sc in 2nd ch from hook, 3 sc in next ch: 4 sc; ch 1, turn.

Row 2: Sc in first sc, 3 sc in next sc: 4 sc; ch 1, turn, leaving rem 2 sc unworked.

Repeat Row 2 until braid is desired length. At end of last row, do not ch or turn. Finish off.

Braid 4

Stitch Guide

Puff Stitch (Pst): Insert hook in specified st or sp and draw up a lp, (YO, insert hook in same specified st or sp and draw up a lp) 2 times; YO and draw through all 6 lps on hook: Pst made.

Instructions

Ch 3.

Row 1: Pst in 3rd ch from hook; ch 1, turn.

Row 2: Pst in same ch as first Pst; ch 1, turn.

Row 3: Pst in center of Pst 2 rows below, inserting hook after first front lp of Pst; ch 1, turn.

Repeat Row 3 until braid is desired length. Finish off.

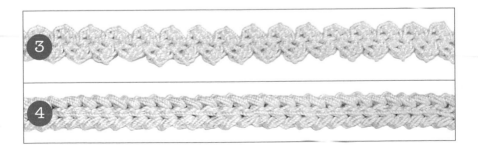

Braid 5

Instructions

Ch 4.

Row 1: Work 3 sc in 2nd ch from hook, 2 sc in next ch, sc in next ch: 6 sc; ch 1, turn.

Row 2: Work 3 sc in first sc, 2 sc in next sc, sc in next sc; ch 1, turn, leaving last 3 sc unworked.

Repeat Row 2 until braid is desired length. At end of last row, do not ch or turn. Finish off.

Braid 6

Instructions

Ch 3.

Row 1: Work 3 sc in 2nd ch from hook, 2 sc in next ch: 5 sc; ch 1, turn.

Row 2: Work 3 sc in first sc, 2 sc in next sc; ch 1, turn, leaving last 3 sc unworked.

Repeat Row 2 until braid is desired length. At end of last row, do not ch or turn. Finish off.

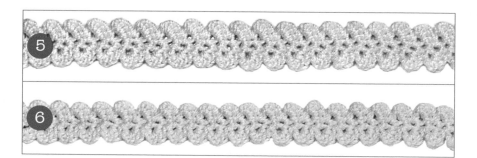

Braid 7

Instructions

Ch 4.

Row 1: Sc in 2nd ch from hook, sc in next ch, 3 sc in last ch: 5 sc; ch 1, turn.

Row 2: Sc in first 2 sc, 3 sc in next sc; ch 1, turn, leaving last 2 sc unworked.

Repeat Row 2 until braid is desired length. At end of last row, do not ch or turn. Finish off.

Braid 8

Instructions

Ch 4.

Row 1: Sc in 2nd ch from hook, skip next ch, 3 sc in last ch: 4 sc; ch 1, turn.

Row 2: Sc in first sc, 3 sc in next sc; ch 1, turn, leaving last 2 sc unworked.

Repeat Row 2 until braid is desired length. At end of last row, do not ch or turn. Finish off.

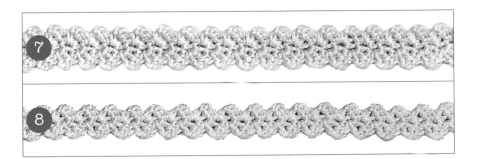

Braid 9

Instructions

Ch 8, join with sl st to form a ring.

Row 1: Ch 1, 10 sc in ring: 10 sc; ch 1, turn.

Row 2: Sc in first sc; *ch 3, sc in next sc; rep from * across: 10 sc and 9 ch-3 sps; ch 8, turn.

Row 3: Skip first 3 ch-3 sps, sc in next ch-3 sp: 1 sc and 1 ch-8 lp; ch 1, turn.

Row 4: Work 10 sc in ch-8 lp: 10 sc; ch 1, turn.

Repeat Rows 2 through 4 until braid is desired length, ending by working a Row 2. At end of last row, do not ch or turn. Finish off.

Braid 10

Instructions

Ch 3; join with sl st to form a ring.

Row 1: Work 5 sc in ring: 5 sc; ch 1, turn.

Row 2: Work 5 sc in back lp of first sc, sl st in both lps of same sc; ch 1, turn.

Repeat Row 2 until braid is desired length. At end of last row, do not ch or turn. Finish off.

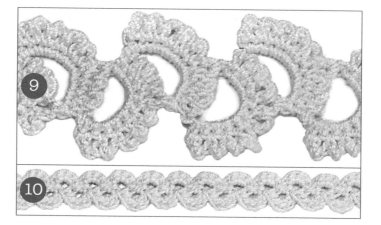

Braid 11

Instructions

Ch 4.

Row 1: Work 4 dc in 4th ch from hook, ch 3, sl st in ch at base of 4 dc; ch 3, turn.

Row 2: Work (4 dc, ch 3, sl st) in ch-3 sp; ch 3, turn.

Repeat Row 2 until braid is desired length. At end of last row, do not ch or turn. Finish off.

Braid 12

Instructions

Ch 5.

Row 1: Work (3 dc, ch 2, 3 dc) in 5th ch from hook; ch 5, turn.

Row 2: Work (3 dc, ch 2, 3 dc) in ch-2 sp; ch 5, turn.

Repeat Row 2 until braid is desired length. At end of last row, do not ch or turn. Finish off.

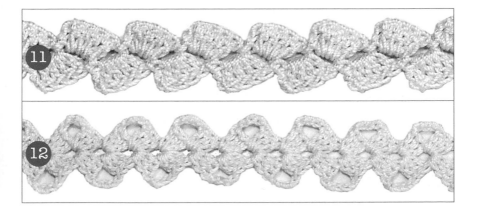

Braid 13

Stitch Guide

Cluster (CL): *YO, insert hook in specified st or sp and draw up a lp to height of a dc, YO and draw through 2 lps on hook; rep from * 2 times more in same st or sp, YO and draw through all 4 lps on hook: CL made.

Instructions

Ch 3.

Row 1: (CL, ch 3, sl st) in 3rd ch from hook; ch 1, turn.

Row 2: Work 6 sc in first ch-3 sp, ch 3, (CL, ch 3, sc) in sp formed by skipped chs at beg of Row 1; ch 1, turn.

Row 3: Work 6 sc in first ch-3 sp, ch 1, (CL, ch 3, sc) in next ch-3 sp; ch 1, turn.

Repeat Row 3 until braid is desired length.

Last Row: Work 6 sc in first ch-3 sp. Finish off.

Braid 14

Instructions

Ch 4.

Row 1: Sc in 2nd ch from hook and in next 2 chs: 3 sc; ch 1, turn.

Row 2: Sc in each sc across; ch 1, turn.

Repeat Row 2 until braid is desired length. At end of last row, do not ch or turn. Finish off.

Braid 15

Instructions

Ch 3.

Row 1: Work (5 dc, ch 3, sc) in 3rd ch from hook; ch 4, turn.

Row 2: (Sc, hdc, 3 dc, tr, ch 3, sc) in ch-3 sp; ch 4, turn.

Repeat Row 2 until braid is desired length. At end of last row, do not ch or turn. Finish off.

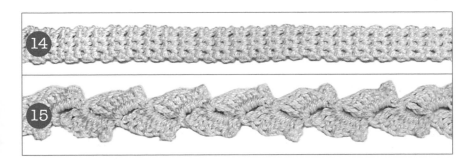

Braid 16

Instructions

Ch 8.

Row 1: Sc in 2nd ch from hook and in next 2 chs, 3 sc in next ch, sc in next 3 chs: 9 sc; ch 1, turn.

Row 2: Skip first sc, sc in back lp of next 3 sc, 3 sc in back lp of next sc, sc in back lp of next 3 sc; ch 1, turn, leaving last sc unworked.

Repeat Row 2 until braid is desired length. At end of last row, do not ch or turn. Finish off.

Braid 17

Instructions

Ch 8.

Row 1: Dc in 4th ch from hook and in next 4 chs: 5 dc; ch 3 (counts as first dc on next row now and throughout), turn.

Row 2: Work 3 dc in first dc, (2 dc in next dc) 3 times, dc in last dc: 11 dc; ch 3, turn.

Row 3: Work 3 dc in first dc, (2 dc in next dc) 3 times, dc in next dc; ch 3, turn, leaving last 6 dc unworked.

Repeat Row 3 until braid is desired length. At end of last row, do not ch or turn. Finish off.

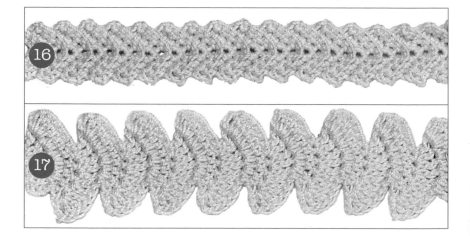

Braid 18

Instructions

Ch 8.

Row 1: Dc in 4th ch from hook and in next 4 chs: 5 dc; ch 4, turn.

Row 2: Sl st in 3rd ch from hook, 3 dc in first dc, (2 dc in next dc) 3 times, dc in last dc: 10 dc; ch 4, turn.

Row 3: Sl st in 3rd ch from hook, 3 dc in first dc, (2 dc in next dc) 3 times, dc in next dc; ch 4, turn, leaving last 5 dc unworked.

Repeat Row 3 until braid is desired length. At end of last row, do not ch or turn. Finish off.

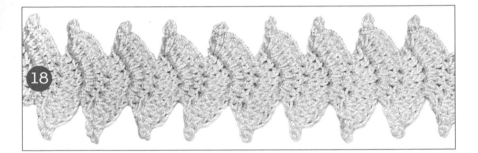

CORDS

Although we've shown our cords worked in size 3 crochet cotton, you'll want to try them in a variety of types and sizes of yarns. Just remember not to use drawstrings in garments for babies or young children because of the danger of strangulation. When used as drawstrings, each end is usually knotted.

1 Slip Stitch Cord

Instructions

Chain the desired length, plus a little extra; sl st in 2nd ch from hook and in each rem ch; finish off. When working the sl sts, be sure to draw each st completely up onto the working part of the hook.

2 Single Crochet Cord

Instructions

Chain the desired length, plus a little extra; sc in 2nd ch from hook and in each rem ch; finish off.

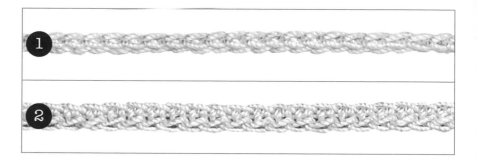

3 Half Double Crochet Cord

Instructions

Chain the desired length, plus a little extra; hdc in 3rd ch from hook and in each rem ch; finish off.

4 Parallel Chain

Instructions

Place loose slip knot on hook, insert hook in bottom of slip knot and draw up a lp; *gently remove one lp from hook and hold base of removed lp so it does not pull out or twist, YO and draw through lp on hook, place removed lp back on hook, YO and draw through one lp on hook; rep from * until chain is desired length.

Note: *This cord is stretchy!*

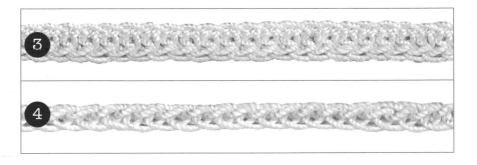

5 Romanian Cord
Instructions

Working loosely, ch 2, sc in top lp of 2nd ch from hook *(Step 1, below)*, turn work 90 degrees clockwise *(Step 2)*, sc in 2 lps on left *(Steps 3, 4 and 5)*; *turn work 90 degrees clockwise *(Step 6)*, sc in 2 lps on left that were formed by sc before last sc made (Step 6); rep from * until cord is desired length *(Step 7)*.

6 Textured Cord
Instructions

Ch 3, pull up lp on hook about ¼" (7 mm), insert hook in 2nd ch from hook and draw up a ¼" (7 mm) lp, insert hook in 3rd ch from hook and draw up a ¼" (7 mm) lp, YO and draw through all 3 elongated lps on hook; pull up lp on hook about ¼" (7 mm), turn work clockwise (to the left), insert hook under top 2 strands and draw up a ¼" (7 mm) lp, insert hook in next

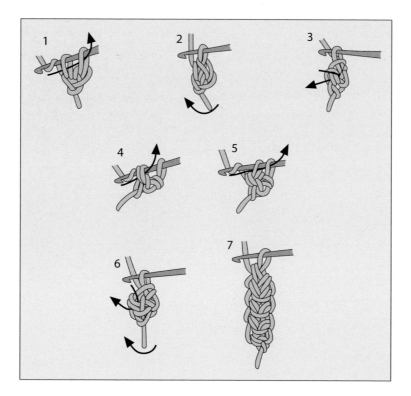

lp to left of last 2 strands and draw up a ¼" (7 mm) lp, YO and draw through all 3 elongated lps on hook; *pull up lp on hook about ¼" (7 mm), turn work clockwise (to the left), insert hook under top 2 strands and draw up a ¼" (7 mm) lp, insert hook under next 3 lps to left of last 2 strands and draw up a ¼" (7 mm) lp, YO and draw through all 3 elongated lps on hook; rep from * until cord is desired length.

7 Round Cord
Instructions
Ch 5.

Rnd 1: Sc in 5th ch from hook and in each rem ch around: 5 sc. Do not join.

Rnd 2: Sc in first sc and in each rem sc around. Do not join.

Rep Rnd 2 until cord is desired length. Sl st in next sc; finish off.

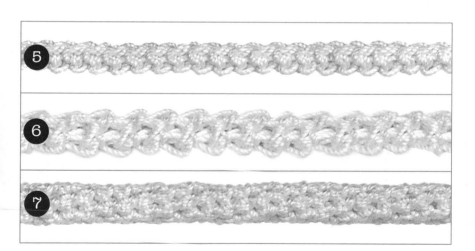

MOTIFS & SHAPES

Motifs come in a variety of shapes and styles, and are excellent accents for many projects. Our motifs range from stars to heraldic symbols. We have also included instructions for basic classic shapes—circles and squares, triangles, pentagons and hexagons.

MOTIFS

Falling Star

Lazy Circle

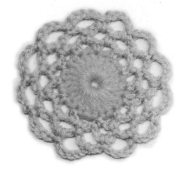

Two colors:
Color A (lime green)
Color B (red)

Two colors:
Color A (yellow)
Color B (pink)

Instructions

With Color A, ch 4, join with sl st to form a ring.

Rnd 1: Ch 1, work 12 sc in ring; join in beg sc. Finish off Color A.

Rnd 2: Join Color B with sc in any sc; *ch 5; sl st in 2nd ch from hook, sc in next ch, hdc in next ch, dc in next ch, skip next sc on Rnd 1, sc in next sc; rep from * around, ending last rep with join with sl st in beg sc. Finish off Color B; weave in yarn ends.

Instructions

With Color A, ch 6, join with sl st to form a ring.

Rnd 1: Ch 3 (counts as a dc), work 23 dc in ring; join with sl st to top of beg ch-3: 24 dc. Finish off Color A.

Rnd 2: Join Color B with sc in any dc; *ch 3, skip next dc, sc in next dc; rep from * around, ending last rep with ch 3; do not join.

Rnd 3: *Sc in next ch-3 lp, ch 4; rep from * around; do not join.

Rnd 4: *Sc in next ch-4 lp, ch 5; rep from * around, ending last rep with sc in beg ch-5 lp. Finish off; weave in yarn ends.

Shield

Two Colors:
Color A (green)
Color B (gold)

Instructions

With Color A, ch 6; join with sl st to form a ring.

Rnd 1: Ch 3 (counts as a dc), in ring work 2 dc, (ch 3, 3 dc) twice, ch 3; join in 3rd ch of beg ch-3. Finish off Color A.

Rnd 2: Join Color B in any ch-3 sp; ch 3 (counts as a dc) in same sp work (2 dc, ch 3, 3 dc) for corner; *dc in each of next 3 dc, in next ch-3 sp work (3 dc, ch 3, 3 dc) for corner; rep from * once more, dc in each of last 3 dc. Finish off Color B.

Rnd 3: Join Color A in first dc of any corner group; ch 3, dc in next 2 dc; *working over Rnd 2 and into ch-3 sp of Rnd 2, work (2 tr, ch 3, 2 tr); dc in each rem 3 dc of corner group; dc in next 6 dc; rep from * 2 times more, dc in last 6 dc. Finish off; weave in yarn ends.

Picot Points

Stitch Guide

Picot: Ch 3, sl st in first ch made: picot made.

Shell: In specified lp work (sc, 4 dc, work picot, 4 dc, sc): shell made.

Instructions

Ch 6, join with sl st to form a ring.

Rnd 1: Sl st in ring, ch 3 (counts as a dc), work 2 dc in ring, work picot; *work 3 dc in ring, work picot; rep from * 4 times more; join with sl st in top of beg ch-3: 18 dc and 6 picots.

Rnd 2: *Sc in next dc; ch 8, skip next dc, next picot and next dc; rep from * 5 times more; join with sl st in beg sc: 6 ch-8 lps.

Rnd 3: *Work shell in next ch-8 lp; rep from * around; join in beg sc: 6 shells. Finish off; weave in yarn ends.

Daisy Wheel

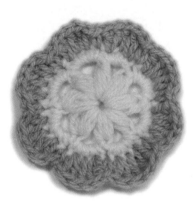

Two colors:
Color A (yellow)
Color B (pink)

Stitch Guide

Puff Stitch (Pst): *YO, insert hook in ring and draw up a lp to height of a dc; rep from * 2 times more, YO and draw through all 7 lps on hook: Pst made.

Instructions

With Color A, ch 6, join with sl st to form a ring.

Rnd 1: Sl st in ring, ch 3; (Pst in ring, ch 3) 8 times, skip beg ch-3; join with sc in top of first Pst.

Rnd 2: *Work 3 sc in next ch-3 sp, sc in top of next Pst; rep from * around, ending last rep with 3 sc in last ch-3 sp; join in beg sc. Finish off Color A.

Rnd 3: Join Color B in sc above any Pst; *2 dc in next sc, dc in next sc, 2 dc in next sc, sc in next sc; rep from * around, ending last rep with join in beg sc. Finish off Color B; weave in yarn ends.

Quadrafoil

Two colors:
Color A (lt brown)
Color B (med brown)

Instructions

With Color A, ch 10; join with sl st to form a ring.

Rnd 1: Ch 3 (counts as a dc), work 23 dc in ring; join with sl st in top of beg ch-3: 24 dc. Finish off Color A.

Rnd 2: Join Color B with sc in any dc, sc in each of next 2 dc, work (sc, ch 7, sc) in next dc; *sc in next 5 dc, work (sc, ch 7, sc) in next dc; rep from * around, ending last rep with sc in last 2 dc; join with sc in beg sc.

Rnd 3: *In next ch-7 lp work (7 dc, ch 3, 7 dc), skip next 2 sc**, sc in next sc, skip next 2 sc; rep from * around, ending last rep at **; join with sl st in beg sc. Finish off; weave in yarn ends.

Golden Wheel

Three colors:
Color A (dk green)
Color B (gold)
Color C (med green)

Stitch Guide
Shell: In specified lp work (3 dc, ch 3, 3 dc): shell made.

Instructions
With Color A, ch 4, join with sl st to form a ring.

Rnd 1: Ch 1, work 8 sc in ring; join with sl st in beg sc. Finish off Color A.

Rnd 2: Join Color B with sc in any sc, sc in same st; work 2 sc in each rem sc around: 16 sc; join in beg sc.

Rnd 3: *Ch 10, sl st in next 2 sc; rep from * around, ending last rep with join in beg sl st. Finish off Color B: 8 ch-10 lps.

Rnd 4: Join Color C with sl st in any ch-10 lp; ch 3, in same lp work (2 dc, ch 3, 3 dc); work shell in each rem ch-10 lp around; join in 3rd ch of beg ch-3. Finish off Color C; weave in yarn ends.

Gold Star

Stitch Guide
Shell: In specified sp work (3 dc, ch 3, 3 dc): shell made.

Instructions
Ch 6, join with sl st to form a ring.

Rnd 1: Ch 3, work 2 dc in ring; (ch 3, 3 dc in ring) 4 times, ch 3; join in 3rd ch of beg ch-3.

Rnd 2: Sl st in each of next 2 dc, sl st in next ch-3 sp; in same sp work (ch 3, 2 dc, ch 3, 3 dc); *ch 1, shell in next ch-3 sp; rep from * around, ending last rep with ch 1; join with sc in top of beg ch-3.

Rnd 3: Sc in next 2 dc; *3 sc in ch-3 sp, sc in next 3 dc, dc in ch-1 sp, sc in next 3 dc; rep from * around, ending last rep with sc in last ch-1 sp; join in beg sc. Finish off; weave in yarn ends.

Octagon

Three colors:
Color A (dk blue)
Color B (yellow)
Color C (med blue)

Stitch Guide
Shell: Work 7 dc in specified st: shell made.

Instructions
With Color A, ch 4, join with sl st to form a ring.

Rnd 1: Sl st in ring; ch 3 (counts as a dc), 15 dc in ring; join in top of beg ch-3: 16 dc. Finish off Color A.

Rnd 2: Join Color B with sc in any dc; *skip next dc, shell in next dc, skip next dc, sc in next dc; rep from * around, ending last rep with sl st in beg sc. Finish off Color B.

Rnd 3: Join Color C with sc in 4th dc of any shell; *ch 3, in next sc work (2 tr, ch 3, 2 tr); ch 3, sc in 4th dc of next shell; rep from * around, ending last rep with join with sc in beg sc.

Rnd 4: Ch 3, sc in same sc; *3 sc in next ch-3 sp, sc in each of next 2 tr, in next ch-3 sp work (sc, ch 3, sc), sc in each of next 2 tr; work 3 sc in next ch-3 sp, in next sc work (2 sc, ch 3, 2 sc) rep from * around, ending last rep with 3 dc in last ch-3 sp; join in beg sc. Finish off Color C; weave in yarn ends.

Be Mine

Two colors:
Color A (red)
Color B (white)

Instructions

Row 1: With Color A, ch 4 (counts as a dc), work 2 dc in 4th ch from hook: 3 dc; ch 3 (counts as first dc of following row), turn.

Row 2: Work 3 dc in next dc, dc in next dc; ch 3, turn: 5 dc.

Row 3: Dc in base of ch, dc in next dc, 3 dc in next dc, dc in next dc, 2 dc in last dc: 9 dc; turn.

Row 4: Sl st in first dc; skip next dc, 5 dc in next dc, skip next dc, sl st in next dc; skip next dc, 5 dc in next dc, skip next dc, sl st in last dc. Do not turn.

Edging: Ch 1, sc evenly in sides of rows through Row 1, work 3 sc in base of center dc of Row 1; sc evenly in sides of rows to Row 4; join with sl st in beg sc. Finish off Color A.

Lacy Border: Join Color B with sl st in center sl st of Row 4; *ch 3, sc in next st; rep from * around; join with sl st in beg sl st. Finish off; weave in yarn ends.

Peacock's Eye

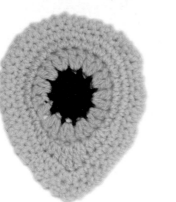

Four colors:

Color A (deep blue)
Color B (lime green)
Color C (tan)
Color D (lt green)

Instructions

Rnd 1: With Color A, ch 4 (counts as first dc of rnd); work 11 dc in 4th ch from hook; join with sl st in top of beg ch-4: 12 dc. Finish off Color A.

Rnd 2: Join Color B in any dc; ch 3 (counts as a dc), dc in same dc; work 2 dc in each rem dc around; join in top of beg ch-3. Finish off Color B.

Rnd 3: Join Color C with sc in any dc, work another sc in same st; work 2 sc in each dc until 6 sts rem; 2 hdc in each of next 2 sts, in next st work (dc, tr), in next st work (tr, dc), in each of next 2 sts work 2 hdc; join with sl st in beg sc of rnd. Finish off Color C.

Rnd 4: Join Color D with sc in same sc as last sl st made; sc in each sc around to dc, work 2 sc in each of next 2 dc, sc in each rem st; join with sl st in beg sc.

Rnd 5: *Ch 2, sl st in next st; rep from * around, ending last rep with ch 2; join in beg sl st. Finish off Color D; weave in yarn ends. Lightly steam piece if needed to keep work flat.

SHAPES

Crochet motifs can be made in just about any shape. Here are five classic shapes that you may find useful.

Note: *All are made with three colors: Color A (yellow), Color B (blue) and Color C (white).*

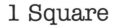

1 Square

Instructions

With Color A, ch 4, join with sl st to form a ring.

Rnd 1: Ch 3 (counts as a dc), 2 dc in ring, (ch 3, 3 dc in ring) 3 times, ch 3; join with sl st in top of beg ch-3: 4 ch-3 sps. Finish off Color A.

Rnd 2: Join Color B with sl st in any ch-3 sp; in same sp work (ch 3, 2 dc, ch 3, 3 dc): corner made; *ch 1, in next ch-3 sp work (3 dc, ch 3, 3 dc): corner made; rep from * 2 times more; ch 1; join with sl st in top of beg ch-3. Finish off Color B.

Rnd 3: Join Color C with sl st in any ch-3 corner sp; in same sp work (ch 3, 2 dc, ch 3, 3 dc); *ch 1, work 3 dc in next ch-1 sp for side, ch 1, in next corner ch-3 sp work (3 dc, ch 3, 3 dc); rep from * 2 times more, ch 1, work 3 dc in last ch-1 sp, ch 1; join with sl st in top of beg ch-3.

Rnd 4: Ch 1, sc in same st as joining; sc in each dc and in each ch-1 sp around, working 3 sc in each ch-3 sp; join with sl st in beg sc. Finish off; weave in yarn ends.

2 Triangle

Instructions

With Color A, ch 4, join with sl st to form a ring.

Rnd 1: Ch 3 (counts as a dc), 2 dc in ring; (ch 3, 3 dc in ring) 2 times, ch 3; join with sl st in top of beg ch-3: 3 ch-3 sps. Finish off Color A.

Rnd 2: Join Color B with sl st in any ch-3 sp; in same sp work (ch 3, 2 dc, ch 3, 3 dc): corner made; *ch 1, in next ch-3 sp work (3 dc, ch 3, 3 dc); rep from * once, ch 1; join with sl st in top of beg ch-3. Finish off Color B.

Rnd 3: Join Color C with sl st in any ch-3 corner sp; in same sp work (ch 3, 2 dc, ch 3, 3 dc); *ch 1, work 3 dc for side in next ch-1 sp; in next ch-3 sp work (3 dc, ch 3, 3 dc); rep from * once, ch 1, 3 dc in next ch-1 sp; join with sl st in top of beg ch-3.

Rnd 4: Ch 1, sc in joining; sc in each dc and in each ch-1 sp around, working 3 sc in each corner ch-3 sp; join with sl st in beg sc. Finish off; weave in yarn ends.

3 Circle

Rnd 4: Ch 1, sc in joining; sc in each dc around; join with sl st in beg sc. Finish off; weave in yarn ends.

4 Pentagon

Instructions

With Color A, ch 4 (counts as a dc).

Rnd 1: Work 11 dc in 4th ch from hook; join with sl st in 4th ch of beg ch-4: 12 dc. Finish off Color A.

Rnd 2: Join Color B with sl st in any dc; ch 3 (counts as a dc), dc in joining; work 2 dc in each dc around: 24 dc; join with sl st in top of beg ch-3. Finish off Color B.

Rnd 3: Join Color C with sl st in any dc; ch 3 (counts as a dc), *2 dc in next dc, dc in next dc; rep from * around: 36 dc; join with sl st in top of beg ch-3.

Instructions

With Color A, ch 5; join with sl st to form a ring.

Rnd 1: Ch 3 (counts as a dc), work 2 dc in ring; (ch 3, work 3 dc in ring) 4 times, ch 3; join with sl st in top of beg ch-3: 5 ch-3 sps. Finish off Color A.

Rnd 2: Join Color B with sl st in any ch-3 sp; in same sp work (ch 3, 2 dc, ch 3, 3 dc): corner made; *ch 1, in next ch-3 sp work (3 dc, ch 3, 3 dc): corner made; rep from * 3 times more; ch 1; join with sl st in top of beg ch-3. Finish off Color B.

Rnd 3: Join Color C with sl st in any ch-3 corner sp; in same sp work (ch 3, 2 dc, ch 3, 3 dc); *ch 1, work 3 dc in next ch-1 sp for side; ch 1, in next corner ch-3 sp work (3 dc, ch 3, 3 dc); rep from * 3 times more, ch 1, work 3 dc in next ch-1 sp, ch 1; join with sl st in top of beg ch-3.

Rnd 4: Ch 1, sc in joining; sc in each dc and in each ch-1 sp around, working 3 sc in each ch-3 sp; join with sl st in beg sc. Finish off; weave in yarn ends.

5 Hexagon

Instructions

With Color A, ch 6; join with sl st to form a ring.

Rnd 1: Ch 3 (counts as a dc), work 2 dc in ring; (ch 3, work 3 dc in ring) 5 times, ch 3; join with sl st in top of beg ch-3: 6 ch-3 sp. Finish off Color A.

Rnd 2: Join Color B with sl st in any ch-3 sp; in same sp work (ch 3, 2 dc, ch 3, 3 dc): corner made; *ch 1, in next ch-3 sp work (3 dc, ch 3, 3 dc): corner made; rep from * 4 times more; ch 1; join with sl st in top of beg ch-3; Finish off Color B.

Rnd 3: Join Color C with sl st in any ch-3 corner sp; in same sp work (ch 3, 2 dc, ch 3, 3 dc); *ch 1, work 3 dc in next ch-1 sp for side, ch 1, in next corner ch-3 sp work (3 dc, ch 3, 3 dc); rep from * 4 times more, ch 1, work 3 dc in last ch-1 sp, ch 1; join with sl st in top of beg ch-3.

Rnd 4: Ch 1, sc in same st as joining; sc in each dc and in each ch-1 sp around, working 3 sc in each ch-3 sp; join with sl st in beg sc. Finish off; weave in yarn ends.

FINAL TOUCHES

Favorite final touches include

curlicues, fringes, and tassels. All are

easy and fun to crochet and make

a project very special. Final touches

put the "wow" factor in your projects.

CURLICUES

These curls are quick and easy to make, and are fun to use on children's clothing, or as a substitute for fringe. They are often used to make doll hair.

They can be made with any yarn, and whatever length you desire.

Curl 1

Instructions

Make a chain of desired length.

Row 1: Work 3 sc in 2nd ch from hook; work 3 sc in each rem ch. Finish off; weave in yarn ends.

Curl 2

Instructions

Make a chain of desired length.

Row 1: Work 2 dc in 4th ch from hook; work 3 dc in each rem ch. Finish off; weave in yarn ends.

Curl 3

Instructions

Make a chain of desired length with first color.

Row 1: Work 2 dc in 4th ch from hook; work 3 dc in each rem ch. Finish off.

Row 2: Starting at top of curl, join contrast yarn with sc in first dc; work sc in each dc across. Finish off; weave in yarn ends.

FRINGE

We most often think of fringe as a finish for afghans, but it actually has many uses. Fringe looks great on pillows and cushions, on rugs, and on children's clothing. Fringe made with crochet cotton can be used on curtains or table runners.

Most patterns state how long to cut the yarn, and how many strands to use in each knot. Generally, cut the strands twice the length you want the finished fringe to be, plus about 2" (5 cm) extra for the knots. Triple knot, or other more elaborate knotting styles, may require 3" (7.5 cm) or 4" (10 cm) extra.

An easy way to make fringe is to find a book close to the length you need, and wind the yarn around that. After you have wound and cut a few fringe pieces, make one or two knots to see if you are happy with the length.

Single Knot Fringe

This is the fringe most often used on afghans. Although any number of strands can be used, 4 strands is usually the minimum.

Hold the specified number of strands for one knot of fringe together, and then fold in half (Step 1, opposite).

Hold the project with the right side facing you. Using a crochet hook, draw the folded ends through the space or stitch from right to wrong side (Step 2).

Pull the loose ends through the folded section (Step 3).

Draw the knot up firmly (Step 4).

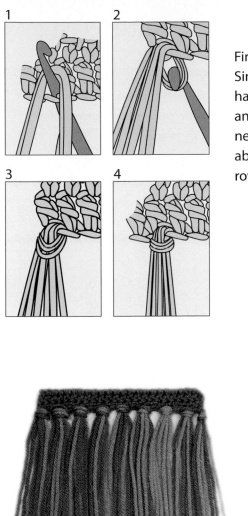

Double Knot Fringe

First work a complete row of Single Knot Fringe, then using half the strands from one knot and half the strands from the next knot, tie a row of knots about 1½" (4 cm) below the first row *(Fig. 1)*.

Fig. 1

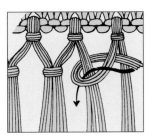

Triple Knot Fringe

First work Double Knot Fringe, then add one more row of knots below *(Fig. 2)*.

Fig. 2

Slanted Triple Knot Fringe

Similar to Triple Knot, the knots are tied by jumping over one more group of strands before tying the knot *(Fig. 3)*.

Fig. 3

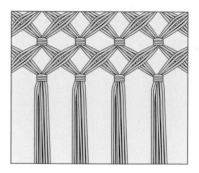

TASSEL

You can mix a variety of materials in a tassel, Including metallic or furry yarns. Here's how to make the basic version.

Basic Tassel

Fig. 1

Cut a piece of cardboard ½" (12 mm) longer than the length desired for the tassel.

Place a 12" (30.5 cm) piece of yarn or cord across the top for the tie and wind yarn around the cardboard and over the tie until you have the desired thickness.

Draw the tie up tightly and knot securely.

Slide off the cardboard and cut yarn at bottom *(Fig. 1)*.

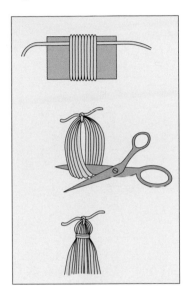

Cut another 12" (30.5 cm) piece of yarn or cord and wrap tightly about an inch below the top of tassel. Wrap several times, then tie a secure knot. Trim ends of cord and bottom of tassel as desired.

A REFRESHER COURSE IN CROCHET

Slip Knot

To begin, make a slip knot (sometimes called a slip loop) on the hook, leaving a 6" (15 cm) tail of yarn *(Fig 1)*.

Fig. 1

Insert the crochet hook and draw the loop onto the hook by pulling on the end marked A *(Fig 2)*.

Fig. 2

The knot should be snug on the hook but should slide easily *(Fig 3)*.

Fig. 3

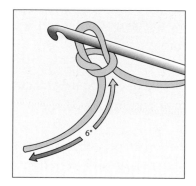

Chain (ch)

The chain is the foundation on which all crochet is built. It is rather like the bottom row of a brick wall.

Hold the hook in your dominant hand and the yarn in the other hand. Take the yarn from back to front over the hook and catch it with the hook head and draw it through the slip knot on the hook *(Fig 4)*.

Fig. 4

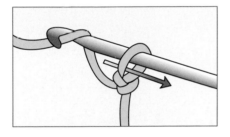

You have now made one chain stitch. Repeat this step for each additional chain required, moving your thumb and index finger up close to the hook after each stitch or two *(Fig 5)*.

Fig. 5

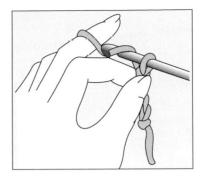

Single Crochet (sc)

First make a chain to the desired length.

Step 1: Insert the hook into the back bump of the 2nd chain from the hook *(Fig 6)*.

Fig. 6

Step 2: Hook the yarn, bringing the yarn over the hook from the back to the front and draw through *(Fig 7)*.

Fig. 7

Step 3: There are now 2 loops on the hook *(Fig 8)*. Take the yarn over the hook again from back to front, hook it and draw through both loops on the hook: one loop now remains on the hook and you have made one sc stitch. To make the next stitch, continue to work in this manner.

Fig. 8

To work additional rows, chain 1 (the turning chain) and turn work counterclockwise.

Skip the turning chain and work one sc in the sc nearest your hook, inserting the hook under the top two loops of the stitch *(Fig 9)*.

Fig. 9

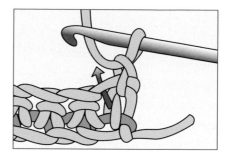

Half Double Crochet (hdc)

Begin by making a chain the desired length.

Step 1: Yarn over the hook. Insert the hook into the back bump of the 3rd chain from the hook; yarn over and draw up a loop: 3 loops are now on the hook.

Step 2: Yarn over again and draw the yarn through all 3 loops on the hook at one time. You have made one hdc stitch *(Fig 10)*.

Fig. 10

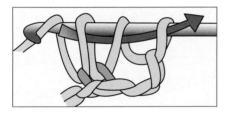

To work additional rows, make 2 chains and turn work counterclockwise. Beginning in 2nd stitch (2 chains count as first half double crochet), work a half double crochet in each stitch across. Work the last stitch into the top chain; chain 1 and turn the work counterclockwise.

Double Crochet (dc)

Begin by making a chain the desired length.

Step 1: Bring the yarn over the hook from back to front, then insert the hook into the back bump of the 4th chain from the hook *(Fig 11)*.

Fig. 11

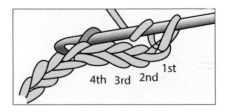

Step 2: Hook the yarn and draw it through. There are now 3 loops on the hook *(Fig 12)*.

Fig. 12

Step 3: Hook the yarn again and draw it through the first two loops on the hook. There are now 2 loops on the hook *(Fig 13)*.

Fig. 13

Step 4: Hook the yarn again and draw it through the remaining 2 loops. You have made one dc stitch.

To work the next dc stitch, repeat Step 1 but insert the hook into the back bump of the next chain rather than the fourth chain from the hook. Repeat Steps 2 through 4 again and continue in this manner across the row.

To work additional rows, make 3 chains and turn work counterclockwise *(Fig 14)*.

Fig. 14

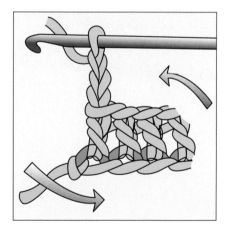

Beginning in 2nd stitch of the previous row (3 chains count as first double crochet), work a double crochet in each stitch *(Fig 15)*.

Fig. 15

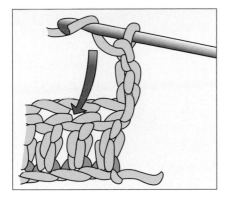

At the end of the row, work the last dc into the top chain of the turning chain of the previous row *(Fig 16)*.

Fig. 16

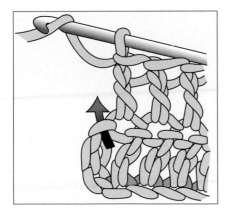

Triple Crochet (tr)

Begin by making a chain the desired length.

Step 1: Bring the yarn over the hook twice. Insert the hook into the back bump of the 5th chain from the hook *(Fig 17)*.

Fig. 17

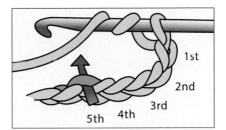

Step 2: Hook the yarn and draw through the chain. There are now 4 loops on the hook *(Fig 18)*.

Fig. 18

Step 3: Hook the yarn again and draw through the first 2 loops on the hook. There are now 3 loops on the hook.

Step 4: Hook the yarn again and draw through the first two loops on the hook. There are now 2 loops on the hook.

Step 5: Hook the yarn and draw through the remaining 2 loops. You have now made one triple crochet stitch *(Fig 19)*.

Fig. 19

To work the next stitches in tr, repeat Steps 1 through 5 in the back bump of each chain, working Step 1 in the next chain rather than the 5th chain from the hook.

Slip Stitch (sl st)

Begin by making a chain the desired length.

Step 1: Insert hook in 2nd chain from the hook. Hook yarn and draw through both stitch and loop in one motion.

Working in a Circle

Begin by making a chain the desired length.

Step 1: Join the stitches with a sl st to form a ring *(Fig 20)*.

Fig. 20

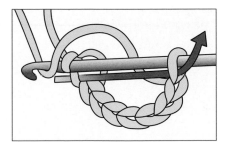

Step 2: Chain the required stitches and work into ring or into the next stitch *(Fig 21)*.

Fig. 21

ABBREVIATIONS & SYMBOLS

Crochet patterns are written in a special shorthand which is used so that instructions don't take up too much space. They sometimes seem confusing, but once you learn them, you'll have no trouble following them.

Abbreviations

Beg	beginning
CL(s)	cluster(s)
Ch(s)	chain(s)
Dc	double crochet
Dec	decrease
Fig	figure
FPdc	front post double crochet
FPsc	front post single crochet
Hdc	half double crochet
Lp(s)	loop(s)
PC	popcorn
Pst	puff stitch
Rem	remaining
Rep	repeat(ing)
Rnd(s)	round(s)
Sc	single crochet
Sl st	slip stitch
Sp(s)	space(s)
St(s)	stitch(es)
Tr	triple crochet
YO	yarn over hook

Standard Symbols

* An asterisk (or double asterisks**) in a pattern row, indicates a portion of instructions to be used more than once. For instance, "rep from * three times" means that after working the instructions once, you must work them again three times for a total of 4 times in all.

: The number of stitches after a colon tells you the number of stitches you will have when you have completed the row or round.